For information address:

24 Wildeoak Ct.,

Columbia, SC 29223

www.contextthinking.com

Introduction

To Future Sages and Gurus bka Brainionaires!

This is a life-changing book for you. The goal is simply show you in summarized form for rapid access to what you need to know about how to manage yourself and enable you to achieve personal and business success in your life by using eight (8) proven business ideas used by the sages and gurus for centuries and are being used today to make millions, even billions of dollars.

This book will give you extraordinary distillation of time-tested wisdom and advanced business ideas and statements to think about that will unconsciously change you; making you into a wiser person in general and wiser business person specifically. When you have finished this book, you will come to the secret of optimal living that is your birthright.

These **secrets** have been known, but kept from the general public because of their dynamic power to shape your thoughts and your future. Now it is available to you today to make the changes you need to be secure/ordered in a World that thinks it is unsecured/chaotic.

You will learn what I call **The Magic 8 Ball** that reveals eight cutting-edge definitive secrets on:

1. **How to be a Better Person**

2. **Leadership**

3. **Strategy**

4. **Entrepreneurship**

5. **Management**

6. **Business Rules and Scorekeeping**

7. **Selling and Marketing**

8. **Innovation and Creativity.**

Let's get started, but first a short story that embodies all of the above areas.

Chapter 1: The Foundation

You are a wise person, setting out through an undiscovered country. You will not depend for the direction of his course upon the hazard of the way. First you will first acquaint yourself with those points (**Indicators**) which are acceptable as fixed and unchangeable, the cardinal points of direction. Then, with compass in hand, you may safely enter the trackless wilderness, for your way is directed by those steadfast **Indicators** which preside alike over the traveled and the untraveled path.

It is my goal when you finish this book, millions of you will find your way from being a slave of your current finances, health, and relationships to freedom in these three areas. The journey will be filled with principles, strategies, objectives, and methods that will help you escape. Right now, you are a slave; your body, time, and very breath belong to a some else. Year after year, you tend their fields and make them richer. Yet, you never tasted the freedom that they enjoy. You never expect to. And yet, something inside lights up when you hear whispers of attempted escape to freedom. Freedom means a hard, dangerous track. Do you try it? Yes, I want to go or no I'll stay where I'm at now. Choose.

You've heard the stories about people who broke free and now return to rescue others. **I am** that former person. Guided by my *"vision"* I hope to never lose a passenger. I want you to follow the North Star to financial, health, and relationship freedom from where you are right now. Follow me.

Every step will seem louder as you walk forward and find three friendly faces; join them. Your head says *yes*, your feet says *no*. If you follow your head, a sure sign that you are on the right path will be a feeling of peace, happiness, and harmony. You may be asking, *if I leave my comfort zone and knock on a strange door will it open and can I trust those who open the door?* Well, "*yes*" is the answer and what you will find is that you're welcomed and will be abundantly fed a buffet.

The buffet is strange foods (knowledge). Food that you've never seen or tasted. Once you've seen and tasted and assimilate it, it will become wisdom for you. You will now realize that the old you is a million miles away, burn the bridge that leads to the old you. You now see a much bigger future before you.

But compass and guiding stars alone are not sufficient to insure a happy outcome of the journey. Preparation and provision are essential that the you may be sustained and strengthened upon the way. You cannot ignore the service of those upon whom you are turning your back.

Even an event with the most careful preparation the end is not assured. You must keep watch over yourself from day to day, lest you overtax your strength and faint before the journey is done, or else tarry too long by the wayside, and so miss the goal at last. You will not rush toward the end of the journey, but will move forward carefully, your course marked by bivouacs of the night and by camps of rest. You will profit by the shade of the wayside. You will leave your pack by the roadway to make pleasant excursions aside. And yet you will be watchful not to linger too long in the pleasant places. Amid the diversions of the way, you will not lose sight of the goal toward which you first set out, and the delays and deviations will but reach forward to the attainment of your goal.

Such a journey every one of us is making. The life which lies before us is an undiscovered country. We are pioneers. Yet we need not be discouraged; we have only to be wise of today's events/actions. There are indicators, cardinal points, of direction which preside infallibly over the ways of life, points fixed for all time and all circumstances, principles of truth. Once we are acquainted with these indicators and are aware of the compass that shows us the way and how to respond to them unfalteringly, we may set out with confidence upon the untried way.

We may not, however, leave behind us the provision that has been laid up in store. For every one of us there has been brought together with great pains a selection of things that will stand us instead in the days to come – these things we cannot afford to leave behind. A great man once said, when he had come to a barrier across his own way: *"I have but one lamp by which my feet are guided, and that is the lamp of self-knowledge. I know of no way of judging of the future but by what I've experienced in the past."*

Setting out with all preparation, we must still be watchful every day, least we squander our strength or fritter the time away. It is not best to set the face steadfastly toward the far-off goal. Especially upon this journey, if it is true that a straight line is not the shortest way. We shall progress with greatest surety by resting now and then; by turning aside for pleasant excursion into some attractive field; by searching out the springs that lie in secluded areas; by tarrying for a season of recreation under the inviting shade. The way of the wise person is not an uninterrupted trail; it is marked by signs of bivouac and camp and excursion. And yet there is a unit of direction and a controlling purpose running through all the days. The ultimate goal must never be lost from sight, and all the diversions of the way must serve but to bring us the more surely to the end of the journey.

You must rely on your own resources, what you know, who you know, when to move, and how far to move, and rest and eat.

The goal of every life must be the realization of its unlimited possibilities operating on an unconscious level.

This powerful little book will have served its aim if it helps to bring you nearer to that goal.

You will reach free state, but keep in mind there are bounty hunters everywhere, select your friends wisely. It will be a long journey and you will get across the veil that covers your freedom. You will make it. It takes courage, luck, help, and stamina. You can now find things, make things, and adapt to things. You have found a heavenly place of financial, health and relationship freedom where you can proudly say:

Free at last!

Chapter 2: The MAGIC 8 Ball for Sages and Gurus

The following information will make you a wiser person by looking at all the proven elements that sages say and have written about that must be known to succeed in business and life. They have the power to renew your soul, put a spark of passion back in you life.

But first, there are four (4) key questions that you must ask yourself as you learn these secrets and apply them to your specific expertise, craft, or industry:

1. Who are the official and unofficial (influential) people who are the leaders in your industry network; professionally and socially? List them.

2. Do these leaders communicate with leaders in other industries that are relevant to their industry and how often do they communicate? Show the network by drawing lines that connect them.

3. How far apart in physical location are the leaders? Show the connection by drawing lines that connect them.

4. What is the level of conversation at the lowest level in the organization and does that conversation have and add value to your bottomline? Listen to the words or industry language being used and assign a weight to it.

Now, read and think on what's presented and you will find the total truth in each. Use these truths that have been used by sages and gurus to prosper and find financial, health, and relationship freedom. They are not long winded ideas, but as you know, quantity is not the key. It's your ability to experience what is presented and paraphrase it in the best way you understand it. That is the key to your transformation to being better, thinking better, and acting better.

A Better You

Now, self-mastery is more of an art than a science. It is the art within the framework in which you live and breathe. A **framework** provides the boundaries, left, right, front, and rear limits that you set for yourself or that is set by outside forces.

This is the key to self-mastery. YOU MUST TAKE THE ROAD LESS TRAVELLED. THAT ROAD IS TO CONSCIOUSLY PUT OTHERS FIRST UNTIL IT BECOMES AN UNCONSCIOUS HABIT. THIS MUST BE DONE DAILY. What you see reflected back to you will then create in you the feelings that you desire. It is not an easy road to follow, because most people naturally put themselves first. Consciously make it a point to praise others, put it on a calendar if need be, until you can do it without thinking and you will experience much success in becoming a master of your self.

Leadership

Now, leadership is more of an art than a science. It is the art within the framework in which you live and breathe. A framework provides the boundaries, left, right, front, and rear limits that you set for yourself or that is set by outside forces. FIRST, KNOW THAT THERE ARE THREE LEVELS OF LEADERSHIP WITHIN THIS FRAMEWORK: STRATEGIC LEADERSHIP ENVIRONMENT (HIGH LEVEL), OPERATIONAL LEADERSHIP ENVIRONMENT (MID LEVEL), AND TACTICAL LEADERSHIP ENVIRONMENT (LOW LEVEL). You have to know how each environment impacts the other because they all operate simultaneously. Most people focus on the tactical environment because it is where the most pain is felt. Some people say stop the pain and I'm fine, but the pain comes again sometimes in greater intensity because the true cause has not been dealt with on the strategic or operational environment.

Secondly, you need to **KNOW WHICH LEADERSHIP ENVIRONMENT YOU ARE CURRENTLY IN.** Here you are looking at what's been been done already that you have access to and how might this information be of use in the future. Then you think about if I use this information, what counter moves will need to made in the other environments to ensure that all the level of leadership are in synchronization with each other.

Third, **WHEN CONFRONTED WITH THE TURBULENT ISSUES OF LIFE AND CHANGE, YOU WILL BE MEASURED BY YOUR SUBORDINATES BY YOUR ABILITY TO REMAIN CALM AT CRITICAL DECISION POINTS.** People follow you because of this trait. You will inspire them to accomplish anything if they see that you have a calm demeanor when all is not going as expected. The way to get them to remain calm is to be able to tell them stories that reflect the

16

values that you want them to display. From these stories, they will glean the wisdom of what it take to be a leader and unconsciously learn to be better leaders even though they are following you.

Strategy

Strategy is more of an art than a science. It is the art within the framework in which you live and breathe. A framework provides the boundaries, left, right, front, and rear limits that you set for yourself or that is set by outside forces. First you must **BE AWARE** THAT THERE ARE STRATEGIC POINTS AND POSITIONS IN THIS FRAMEWORK. THERE ARE YOUR CUSTOMERS, SUPPLIERS, COMPETITORS, ALTERNATIVES, AND BARRIER TO ENTRY STRATEGIC POINTS. You've got to understand how all these points work together and how your organization's strategic points work in line with theirs. Most people do not know the strategic points of their customers to any barriers to entry. They might be successful, but they can be more successful if they take the time to find out these points. Finally, once you know these points, then you can **leverage your competitive advantages, position, and strategic points. You can do this by taking the values and people based ACTION that creates TRUST** among those in your strategic environment.

Entrepreneurship

Entrepreneurship is more of an art than a science. It is the art within the framework in which you live and breathe. A framework provides the boundaries, left, right, front, and rear limits that you set for yourself or that is set by outside forces. Entrepreneurship deals with the internal practices within an organization.

This is the key to entrepreneurship is to START A BUSINESS WHERE YOU KNOW THE INDUSTRY STANDARDS, CENTER-POINTS, AND WHY THE BUSINESS EXISTS. YOU MUST ALSO SPEAK THE LANGUAGE (TECHNICAL AND ENTREPRENEURIAL JARGON. Now here is the kicker, in order to have *superior performance* in entrepreneurship, you've got to *know what you are good at and communicate how to maximize return on investment.*

Management

Management is more of an art than a science. It is the art within the framework in which you live and breathe. A framework provides the boundaries, left, right, front, and rear limits that you set for yourself or that is set by outside forces. Management deals with the internal practices within an organization.

This is the key to mastering management is to FOCUS ON YOUR BUSINESS FINANCIAL STRENGTHS. THOSE STRENGTHS ARE SHOWN THROUGH ITS PEOPLE, PROCESSES, SYSTEMS, AND TASKS THAT ARE PERFORMED DAILY IN ANY COMPANY. YOU GOT TO TIE SPECIFIC METRICS THAT LINK PEOPLE, PROCESSES, SYSTEMS, AND TASKS TOGETHER. Where do you find these metrics? They are the financial statement, cash flow, balance sheet, net revenue, and return on investment (ROI). By focusing on these metrics and linking them to the key areas above, *you will be able to manage who needs what when.* Now here is the kicker, in order to have *superior performance* in management, you've got to *show how everyone who works for you has stock in the output/outcome in your organization.* Show them by keeping an open book mentality when it comes to the financial metrics of the organization. Let them know what position the company is in.

Business Rules and Scorekeeping

Business rules and scorekeeping is more of an art than a science. It is the art within the framework in which you live and breathe. A framework provides the boundaries, left, right, front, and rear limits that you set for yourself or that is set by outside forces. Business rules and scorekeeping deals with the internal practices within an organization.

This is the key to business rules and scorekeeping is to LEARN HOW USE ECONOMICS (SUPPLY AND DEMAND) DAILY IN ACCOUNTING FOR WHEN TO ASSOCIATE COST AS THEY RELATE TO REVENUE AND SALES. YOU HAVE TO KNOW THE FINANCIAL INFORMATION/ METRICS AND MAKE SURE THAT THEY ARE COMMONLY USED AND ARE BASED ON THE LIFE-CYCLE STAGES IN THE BUSINESS. YOUR GOAL SHOULD BE GROWTH IN

MARKET SHARE OR SALES. IF YOU ARE IN A MATURE MARKET, YOU MUST REDUCE COSTS AND OPERATING EXPENSES, FOCUS ON CUSTOMER SATISFACTION AND RETENTION. Now here is the kicker, in order to have *superior performance* in business rules and scorekeeping, you've got to *understand these rules and scorekeeping in operations, services, or products separately.*

Selling and Marketing

Selling and Marketing is more of an art than a science. It is the art within the framework in which you live and breathe. A framework provides the boundaries, left, right, front, and rear limits that you set for yourself or that is set by outside forces. Selling and Marketing deals with the internal practices within an organization.

This is the key to selling and marketing is to **HAVE YOUR CUSTOMERS UNCONSCIOUSLY VIEW YOUR PRODUCT/SERVICE POSITIVELY BY BRAND BUILDING AND CREATE LOYALTY BY USE OF PICTURES THAT ARE REPETITIVELY PLACED BEFORE THEM THAT DIFFERENTIATES YOUR PRODUCT OR SERVICE (NICHE) TO CREATE TRUST, COMMUNALITY, AND GROWTH.** Now here is the kicker, in order to have *superior performance* in selling and marketing, you've got to *focus the customer on the adoption curve of your product or service.*

Innovation and Creativity

Innovation and creativity is more of an art than a science. It is the art within the framework in which you live and breathe. A framework provides the boundaries, left, right, front, and rear limits that you set for yourself or that is set by outside forces. Innovation and creativity deals with the internal practices within an organization.

This is the key to innovation and creativity is to KNOW CREATION IS LIMITED BY MENTAL ROADBLOCKS OF ASSUMPTIONS WE CARRY WITH US. YOU MUST LEARN TO LOOK BEYOND YOUR ASSUMPTIONS BY BEING MORE OBSERVANT OF COUNTER-INTUITIVE INSIGHTS THAT ARE GAINED FROM LOOKING AT WHAT WORKS BEST AND AT THE BEST IDEAS EXIST. Now here is the kicker, in order to have *superior performance* in innovation and creativity, you've got to *use words and images to get a mental picture to generate more ideas and thus improve the quality of your innovative and creative thinking.*

About The Author

Dr. Joseph W. Graham, Ph. D., Business Administration, BS in Graphic Design. He served in Operation Desert Storm, Operation Restore Democracy in Haiti, and Operation Enduring and Iraqi Freedom. His highest military award is the Bronze Star Medal. He currently works as a Publisher. He has published over 75 books/ebooks.

He's known as one of the world's unified thinkers and founder of a breakthrough   thinking method called Context Thinking.

Full Professional Biography

A 10-year veteran of the context thinking field, Joseph Graham is unique among experts as the man who's actually developed and executed the day-to-day thinking strategies.

Today, he's the #1 best selling author of Master The Art of Context Thinking, The 11 Golden Principles of Context Thinking, Sense & Respond: Thinking at a 24/7 Pace, Thinking Quadrant: How to Think on Your Feet Even When You're Sitting, and many others, published worldwide.

Dr. Graham speaks annually to entrepreneurs, independent sales professionals, corporate employees and industry association members on the principles of context thinking.

As one of America's most respected authorities in the knowledge products industry, he also helps achievers who are experts in their field attain worldwide status and million-dollar incomes by developing their thinking around their business strategies, training concepts, industry expertise and unique market posture using context thinking.

Dr. Graham lives in Columbia, South Carolina.

Other information can be found at www.contextthinking.com.

If you need assistance in publishing or marketing your books/ebooks, contact us at:

http://www.emarketingdept.com/services/ebook-publishing.html

http://www.emarketingdept.com/services/marketing-your-book-on-amazon.html